THE FUNNIEST CHRISTMAS JOKE BOOK EVER

By Joe King

Illustrated by Nigel Baines

London SW1V 2SA
www.andersenpress.co.uk

Text copyright © Andersen Press Ltd., 2012
Illustrations copyright © Nigel Baines, 2012

British Library Cataloguing in
Publication Data available.

ISBN 978 1 849 39508 3

Printed and bound in Great Britain by
CPI Group (UK) Ltd, Croydon, CR0 4YY

Santa
Claus

How does Father Christmas climb up a chimney?

He uses a ladder in the stocking.

**Why did Father Christmas
start sneezing as he went
down the chimney?**

Because he had the flue.

**What did Santa say when
Mrs Claus asked about the
weather?**

'Looks like rain, dear.'

**What does Father Christmas
wear on his head to
keep warm?**

A polar ice cap.

What goes, 'Oh! oh! oh!'?

*Father Christmas walking
backwards.*

Who looks after Father Christmas when he's ill?

The National Elf Service.

Father Christmas's sledge broke down on Christmas Eve. He flagged down a passing car and asked, 'Can you help me fix my sledge?' 'Sorry,' replied the driver, 'I'm not a mechanic, I'm a foot doctor.' 'Well then, can you give me a tow?'

Why did Santa get a parking ticket?

He left his sleigh in a 'snow parking zone'.

How do you know Father Christmas is such a good racing driver?

He's always in pole-position.

One year Father Christmas lost his pants!

That's how he got the name Saint-Nickerless.

What do you call a man who claps at Christmas?

Santapplause.

What do you get if you cross Father Christmas with a detective?

Santa Clues.

Why does Father Christmas have a garden?

Because he likes to ho-ho-ho.

What do you call a smelly Santa?

Farta Christmas.

What do you call people who are afraid of Santa?

Claus-trophobic.

What do you get if you cross Father Christmas with a flying saucer?

A UF ho ho ho.

What do you get if you cross Father Christmas with a duck?

A Christmas quacker.

How many presents can Father Christmas fit in an empty sack?

Just one – after that it's not empty any more.

What do you say when Father Christmas is taking the register?

'Present.'

What says, 'ho-ho-whoosh', 'ho-ho-whoosh'?

Father Christmas caught in a revolving door.

What smells most in a chimney?

Father Christmas's nose.

**What's fat and jolly and
runs on eight wheels?**

Father Christmas on roller skates.

**What's red and white and red
and white and red and white
and red and white?**

*Father Christmas rolling
down a hill.*

Why does Father Christmas go down the chimney?

Because it soots him.

How many chimneys does Father Christmas go down?

Stacks.

Father Christmas lost his umbrella, but he didn't get wet. Why not?

Because it wasn't raining.

Reindeer

Did Rudolph go to school?

No, he was elf-taught.

What do reindeer say before telling a joke?

'Listen carefully, this one will sleigh you.'

Why did the reindeer wear sunglasses to the beach?

He didn't want to be recognised.

What do reindeer have that no other animals have?

Baby reindeer.

If a reindeer lost his tail, where would he go for a new one?

A re-tail shop.

Which reindeer has the worst manners?

Rude-olph.

How do you know if there's a reindeer in your fridge?

Look for hoof prints in the butter.

Why do the reindeer love Father Christmas so much?

Because he fawns over them.

Why did Father Christmas call two of his reindeer 'Edward'?

Because two Ed's are better than one, of course.

How can Santa's sleigh possibly fly through the air?

You would too if you were pulled by flying reindeer.

How do you get into Rudolph's house?

Ring the deer-bell.

How does Rudolph know when Christmas is coming?

He looks at his calen-deer.

What's the difference between a reindeer and a biscuit?

You can't dunk a reindeer in your tea.

What is Rudolph's favourite day of the year?

Red Nose Day.

Why is Rudolph so good at trivia?

*Because he nose a lot
and is very bright.*

Why do reindeer wear fur coats?

*Because they'd look ridiculous
in plastic macs.*

Why is Prancer always wet?

Because he's a rain-deer.

How would you get four reindeer in a car?

*Two in the front and two
in the back.*

And how would you get four polar bears in a car?

Take the reindeer out first.

'I'm so strong I could lift a reindeer with one hand.'

'Yeah, but where are we going to find a one-handed reindeer?'

What do reindeer hang on their Christmas trees?

Horn-aments.

OK... but I get to keep the travel sweets.

What does Father Christmas call the blind reindeer?

No-eye-deer.

What does Father Christmas call that three-legged reindeer?

Eileen.

What does Father Christmas call the blind reindeer with only three legs?

Still no-eye-deer.

What did the reindeer say to the elf?

Nothing, reindeer can't talk.

'What has antlers, pulls Father Christmas's sleigh and is made of cement?'

'I don't know.'

'A reindeer.'

'What about the cement?'

'I just threw that in to make it hard.'

Which reindeer can jump higher than a house?

They all can. Houses can't jump.

Elves

How would you
describe a rich elf?

Welfy.

How long should an elf's legs be?

Just long enough to reach the ground.

Who is Santa's most famous elf?

Elfvis.

How many elves does it take to change a light bulb?

Ten. One to change the light bulb and nine to stand on each other's shoulders.

If athletes get athlete's foot, what do elves get?

Mistle-toes.

Why did the elf push his bed into the fireplace?

Because he wanted to sleep like a log.

If there were eleven elves, and another one came along, what would he be?

The twelf.

What do elves use to go from floor to floor?

An elfevator.

Why was Santa's little helper depressed?

Because he had low elf-esteem.

What do elves write on Christmas cards?

Have a fairy happy Christmas.

What is a female elf called?

A shelf.

Why did Santa tell off one of his elves?

Because he was goblin his Christmas dinner.

Presents

'Can I have a broken drum for Christmas?'

'The best thing you could have asked for. You can't beat it.'

'Can I have a puppy for Christmas?'

'Certainly not! You can have turkey just like everyone else.'

'Can I have a wombat for Christmas?'

'What would you do with a wombat?'
'Play wom, of course.'

How do you make opening your Christmas presents last longer?

Open them with boxing gloves on.

Who is a child's favourite king?

Stoc-King

Dear Father Christmas, Please may I have a yellow door? From Sherlock Holmes.

Watson: 'Why do you want a yellow door, Sherlock?'

Sherlock: 'Lemon-entry, my dear Watson.'

Dear Father Christmas, Could you please send me some crocodile shoes?

Father Christmas: 'Can't do that. He hasn't said what size shoes his crocodile wears.'

What do wizards use to wrap their presents?

Spell-o-tape.

What did the farmer get for Christmas?

A cow-culator.

What did the dog get for Christmas?

A mobile bone.

Christmas Dinner Jokes

What beats his chest and swings from Christmas cake to Christmas cake?

Tarzipan.

Who is never hungry at Christmas?

The turkey – he's always stuffed.

What's the best thing to put into a Christmas cake?

Your teeth.

'We had Grandma for
Christmas dinner this year.'

'Really? We had turkey.'

**Why did the Christmas cookie
go to the doctor?**

He was feeling crummy.

**What do vampires put on
their turkey at Christmas?**

Grave-y.

**Mother bought a huge turkey
for Christmas dinner.
'That must have cost
a fortune!' I said.**

**'Actually I got it for a poultry
amount,' she said.**

How do you tell the difference between a turkey and tinned custard?

Look at the label.

**Last year's Christmas
pudding was so awful
I threw it in the sea.**

*That's probably why
the ocean's full of currants.*

**How do you make
Father Christmas stew?**

*You keep him waiting
for half an hour.*

**'This turkey tastes
like an old sofa!'**

*'Well, you asked for something
with plenty of stuffing.'*

**What did the custard say
to the trifle?**

''Tis the season to be jelly.'

**What do ducks do before
Christmas dinner?**

Pull their Christmas quackers.

What do you drain Christmas-dinner Brussels sprouts with?

An advent colander.

What's the most common wine at Christmas?

I don't like Brussels sprouts.

'Will the turkey be long?'

'No, I think it will be the usual turkey shape.'

Why is turkey so fashionable at Christmas?

Because it's so well dressed.

Christmas Animal Jokes

What position does the Christmas turkey play in rounders?

First baste.

**What do angry mice
send each other?**

Cross-mouse cards.

**What do fish do to
celebrate Christmas?**

They put reefs on the door.

**What do you get when you
cross a bell with a skunk?**

Jingle smells.

**What is white, lives at
the North Pole and
runs around naked?**

A polar bare.

**What kind of pine has
the sharpest needles?**

A porcupine.

Why don't penguins fly?

Because they don't fit into the pilot hats.

What is green, covered with tinsel and goes 'ribbet ribbet'?

A mistle-toad.

What's white, furry and smells of mint?

A polo bear.

What do wild animals sing at Christmas time?

*'Jungle-bells, jungle-bells,
jungle all the way.'*

What do you call a cat on the beach at Christmas?

Sandy Claws.

What kind of bird can write?

A PEN-guin.

Why do birds fly south for the winter?

Because it's too far to walk.

Where do polar bears go to vote?

The North Poll.

43

What do sheep say to Father Christmas?

'Season's bleatings.'

What do you call a penguin wearing ear muffs?

Anything! He can't hear you.

Who delivers Christmas presents to pets?

Santa Paws.

What is six metres tall, has sharp teeth and says, 'Ho ho ho'?

Tyranno-santa Rex.

What's the most boring animal?

A polar bore.

**What sort of insects
love snow?**

Mo-ski-toes.

**What food do you get when
you cross a snowman
with a polar bear?**

A brrrr-grrrrr.

**What do you call a
penguin in the Sahara?**

Lost.

**How do cats greet each
other at Christmas?**

*A furry merry Christmas and
a happy mew year.*

What is a monkey's favourite carol?

King Kong Merrily on High.

Who delivers Christmas presents to elephants?

Elephanta Claus.

Christmas Complaints

'Doctor Doctor, I keep
thinking I'm a Christmas bell!'

*'Just take these pills. If they don't
work give me a ring.'*

'Doctor Doctor, Father Christmas gives us oranges every Christmas. Now I think I'm turning into one!'

'Have you tried playing squash?'

And then I lost my job at the orange juice factory because I couldn't concentrate...

'Nurse! I want to operate. Take this patient to the theatre.'

'Oh good, I love a nice pantomime at Christmas.'

Father Christmas: 'Doctor Doctor, I feel so unfit!'

Doctor: 'You need to go to an elf-farm.'

'Doctor Doctor, with all the excitement of Christmas I can't sleep.'

'Try lying on the edge of your bed. You'll soon drop off.'

Knock Knock

Knock Knock
Who's there?
Mary.
Mary who?
Mary Christmas.

Knock Knock

Who's there?

Avery.

Avery who?

Avery merry Christmas.

Knock Knock

Who's there?

Snow.

Snow who?

Snow business like show business.

Knock Knock

Who's there?

Carol singers!

Carol singers? Do you know what time of night it is?

No, but if you hum it, we'll sing it.

Knock knock

Who's there?

Rabbit.

Rabbit who?

Rabbit up neatly, it's a present.

Knock knock
Who's there?
Arthur.
Arthur who?
Arthur any mince pies left?

Knock knock
Who's there?
Wendy.
Wendy who?
Wendy red red robbin comes bob bob bobbin along.

Knock Knock

Who's there?

Wanda.

Wanda who?

Wanda know what you're getting for Christmas?

Knock Knock

Who's there?

Wayne.

Wayne who?

Wayne in a manger.

Knock Knock

Who's there?

Wenceslas.

Wenceslas who?

Wenceslas train home?

Knock Knock

Who's there?

Doughnut.

Doughnut who?

Doughnut open till Christmas.

Knock Knock
Who's there?
Oakham.
Oakham who?
Oakham all ye faithful.

Knock Knock
Who's there?
Holly.
Holly who?
Holly-days are here again.

Knock Knock
Who's there?
Tree.
Tree who?
Tree wise men.

Knock Knock
Who's there?
Anita.
Anita who?
Anita lift please, Rudolph.

Knock Knock

Who's there?

Yuletide.

Yuletide who?

**Yuletide yourself over with
a snack before dinner.**

Knock Knock

Who's there?

Justin.

Justin who?

**Justin time to deliver
the presents.**

Knock Knock

Who's there?

Coal.

Coal who?

**Coal me if you hear
Santa coming.**

Knock Knock

Who's there?

Snow.

Snow who?

**Snow use – I've forgotten
my name again.**

Knock Knock

Who's there?

Honda.

Honda who?

Honda first day of Christmas my true love sent to me a partridge in a pear tree.

Christmas Crackers

What did Adam say on the day before Christmas?

'It's Christmas, Eve.'

How do you make an idiot laugh on Boxing Day?

Tell him a joke on Christmas Eve.

What does Father Christmas suffer from if he gets stuck in a chimney?

Santa claustrophobia.

What do you have in December that you don't have in any other month?

The letter 'D'.

What do you call a letter sent up the chimney on Christmas Eve?

Black mail.

Who delivers cats' Christmas presents?

Santa Paws.

What says, 'Now you see me, now you don't, now you see me, now you don't'?

A snowman on a zebra crossing.

What do snowmen eat for breakfast?

Frosties.

What did one snowman say to the other snowman?

'Can you smell carrots?'

Why did the little girl change her mind about buying her grandmother a pack of hankies for Christmas?

Because she couldn't work out what size her nose was.

What's a good seasonal tip?

Never catch snowflakes on your tongue until all the birds have flown south for the winter.

What do you call an old snowman?

Water.

What happens if you're naughty before Christmas?

Yule be sorry.

What is the first step in using a Christmas computer?

First, yule log on.

What are red and green and grow on the ocean floor?

Christmas corals.

What kind of money do they use at the North Pole?

Cold cash.

Which Christmas carol never gets sung?

The Second Noel.

What do you call a bunch of chess players bragging about their games in a hotel lobby?

Chess nuts boasting in an open foyer.

How do you scare a snowman?

With a hairdryer.

I wasn't scared. I...er...just melted a little...

When does Christmas come before Halloween?

When you look them up in the dictionary.

Why was the computer so quiet on Christmas Eve?

Not a creature was stirring, not even a mouse.

What did Mary Poppins want for Christmas?

Supercalifragilisticexpially- snowshoes.

What winter sport do trees participate in?

Alpine skiing.

Why was the manger so crowded?

Because of the three wide men.

What is an ig?

An eskimo's house without a loo.

If I'm standing at the North Pole, facing the South Pole, and the East is on my left hand, what's on my right hand?

Fingers.

'Waiter! Waiter! My Christmas pudding is off!'

'Off? Where to?'

What do you get hanging from Father Christmas's roof?

Tired arms.

What do you get if you cross an archer with a gift wrapper?

Ribbon Hood.

**What is the difference
between the Christmas alphabet
and the ordinary alphabet?**

*The Christmas alphabet
has no 'L'.*

**What's brown and sneaks
around the kitchen?**

Mince spies.

How do Christmas trees keep themselves fresh?

They suck an ornamint.

Why is it always cold at Christmas?

Because it's in Decemberrrrrrrrrrrrrr.

What comes at the end of Christmas Day?

The letter 'Y'.

What did one Christmas light say to the other Christmas light?

You light me up.

What is white and goes up?

A confused snowflake.

What do you get if you eat
Christmas decorations?

Tinselitus.

What did the bald man say when he got a comb for Christmas?

'Thanks, I'll never part with it.'

What's Christmas called in the United Kingdom?

Yule Britannia.

Where does mistletoe go to become famous?

Hollywood.

Why do mummies like Christmas so much?

Because of all the wrapping.

What often falls at the North Pole, but never hurts itself?

Snow.

**Did you hear about
the cracker's
Christmas party?**

It went with a bang.

**What did one angel say
to the other?**

'Halo there.'

Songs

What's a hairdressers's favourite Christmas carol?

'Oh Comb All Ye Faithful'.

How does Good King Wenceslas like his pizza?

Deep pan, crisp and even.

**What's a dog's favourite
Christmas song?**

'Deck the Howls'.

**What's a football supporter's
favourite Christmas song?**

'Yule Never Walk Alone'.

What's a rabbit's favourite Christmas carol?

'Lettuce with a Gladsome Mind'.

What's a talkative princess's favourite Christmas carol?

'Silent Knight'.

What do snowmen sing to Father Christmas?

'Freeze a Jolly Good Fellow'.

What's a farmer's favourite Christmas song?

'I'm Dreaming of a Wheat Christmas.'

Twinkle, twinkle
chocolate bar,
Santa drives a rusty car.
Press the starter,
Press the choke.
Off he goes in a
cloud of smoke!

Jingle Bells, Batman smells,
Robin flew away. Father
Christmas lost his knickers,
On the motorway . . . Hey!

While shepherds washed
their socks by night,
And hung them on the line,
The angel of the Lord
came down,
And said, 'Those socks
are mine!'

85

We THREE kings of
Orient are,
Tried to smoke a
rubber cigar,
It was loaded and
exploded . . .

We TWO kings of
Orient are,
Tried to smoke a
rubber cigar,
It was loaded and
exploded . . .

I, ONE king of
Orient are,
Tried to smoke a
rubber cigar,
It was loaded and
exploded . . .

Silent night . . .

Christmas
Book Titles

The Art of Kissing,
by Miss L Toe

Winning at Charades,
by Victor Ree

Guessing your Presents,
by P King

Bad Gifts,
by M. T. Box

How to Receive a Great Present,
by B Good

**What to do After
Christmas Dinner,**
by Clare Inup

101 Cures for Indigestion,
by Ivor Pain

The Twelfth Month,
by Dee Sember

Sledging for Beginners,
by I. C. Bottom

Christmas Questions,
by I Dunnoe & Noah Little

**Make your Parents Buy
you Everything,
*by Ruth Lesschild***

Surprise Presents!
by Omar Gosh

**I'd Rather Have Fish
for Christmas Dinner,
*by Ann Chovie***

**My Brother Hogs
all the Potatoes,
*by Dick Tator***

Christmas
Equations

**Musical instrument + Reindeer =
Organ donor**

**Christmas carol + Money =
Jingle bills**

**Snow + Frankenstein =
Snowball fright**

**Really quiet + Armed crusader =
Silent knight**

**Reindeer + Cows =
Sleigh bulls**

**Rope + 24th December =
The knot before Christmas**